NATIONS IN CONFLICT
AFGHANISTAN

by PEGGY J. PARKS

BLACKBIRCH®
PRESS

San Diego • Detroit • New York • San Francisco • Cleveland • New Haven, Conn. • Waterville, Maine • London • Munich

Photo credits: cover, pages 6, 13, 23, 25, 27, 28, 30, 34, 37, 38, 39, 42-43 © CORBIS; pages 8, 32, 41 © AP Wide World; pages 11, 35 © Getty Images; page 12 © Art Resource; pages 15, 19, 21 © Hulton Archive; page 18 © The Art Archive

LIBRARY OF CONGRESS CATALOGING-IN-PUBLICATION DATA

Parks, Peggy J., 1951-
   Afghanistan / by Peggy J. Parks
        p. cm. — (Nations in conflict series)
      Summary: Describes the geography, history, people and culture, political situation, and future possibilities of Afghanistan.
      Includes bibliographical references and index.
      ISNB 1-56711- 499-7 (hardback : alk paper)
      1. Afghanistan — Juvenile literature. [1. Afghanistan.]
I. Title. II. Series.
DS351.5.P37 2003
958.1—dc21
                                                                        2002010703

CONTENTS

INTRODUCTION: A Battered Country 4

CHAPTER ONE: Place, People, Past 7

CHAPTER TWO: Political Turmoil 19

CHAPTER THREE: Looking to the Future 33

Important Dates 44

For More Information 46

Source Quotations 47

Index 48

A Battered Country

There was a time when Afghanistan was considered one of the most enchanting, beautiful places on earth. One woman who lived and worked there during the 1950s described the country this way: "There was an edge of excitement ... a glimpse of possibilities just waiting to be grasped. ... The excitement lay in that sense of splendid hopes and significant accomplishments lying just ahead, within momentary reach, and a feeling that hands were already being stretched out to achieve them. In that one night Afghanistan ceased to be only a landscape to me: it became a people, a past, and, above all, a future."[1]

In the fifty years since the author wrote those words, Afghanistan has changed. It is now a shattered, poverty-stricken country that barely resembles what it was in years past.

Throughout history, life has never been easy for Afghanistan's people. Long, cold winters in the mountainous areas made travel and communication difficult. Extremely hot and dry summers, severe droughts, and frequent earthquakes posed a constant risk. Unstable, unpredictable governments caused ongoing political problems. Yet in spite of these and other overwhelming obstacles, Afghans—united in their Islamic faith and their loyalty toward their country—have continued to survive.

The year 1978 marked the beginning of two decades of conflict and

violence in Afghanistan. A Communist group overthrew the country's government in a violent coup, and thousands of Afghans were either imprisoned or killed. Then in 1979, the Soviet Union invaded Afghanistan. During nine years of Soviet occupation, millions of Afghans were killed, injured, or forced to leave their homes to seek refuge in other countries. Even after the Soviets were finally driven out of Afghanistan, the war did not end. Instead, the country—which had been politically divided for many years—erupted into civil war, and Afghan rebels fought against each other for power and control.

The story of Afghanistan is one of conflict and crisis, destruction and violence, hope and courage. The country has endured more suffering than almost any place in the world, yet somehow its people manage to go on. Afghanistan is indeed a battered nation—one whose best hope for the future is to draw on the strength of its past.

CHAPTER ONE

Place, People, Past

Afghanistan is located on the continent of Asia, in an area known as the Middle East. The countries around it include Iran, China, and six other countries that, along with Afghanistan, are sometimes called the "Stans:" Pakistan, Kazakhstan, Kyrgyzstan, Tajikistan, Turkmenistan, and Uzbekistan. Before 1991, the only Stans that existed were Afghanistan and Pakistan; the other five countries were part of the Soviet Union.

Afghanistan is about the same size as the state of Texas, and much of its 250,000 square miles are extremely mountainous. The massive Hindu Kush mountain range runs from east to west, and is the tallest of all mountain ranges in the Middle East.

Surviving the Elements

As in other mountainous countries, earthquakes happen often in Afghanistan. The country is crisscrossed with fault lines—natural breaks in the earth's crust. Along these fault lines, large landmasses called plates join together and rub against each other. One of Afghanistan's most devastating earthquakes occurred in March 2002, in the Hindu Kush region. Thousands of people were injured or killed, and thousands more were left homeless.

Many Afghans live in mud-brick houses like this one.

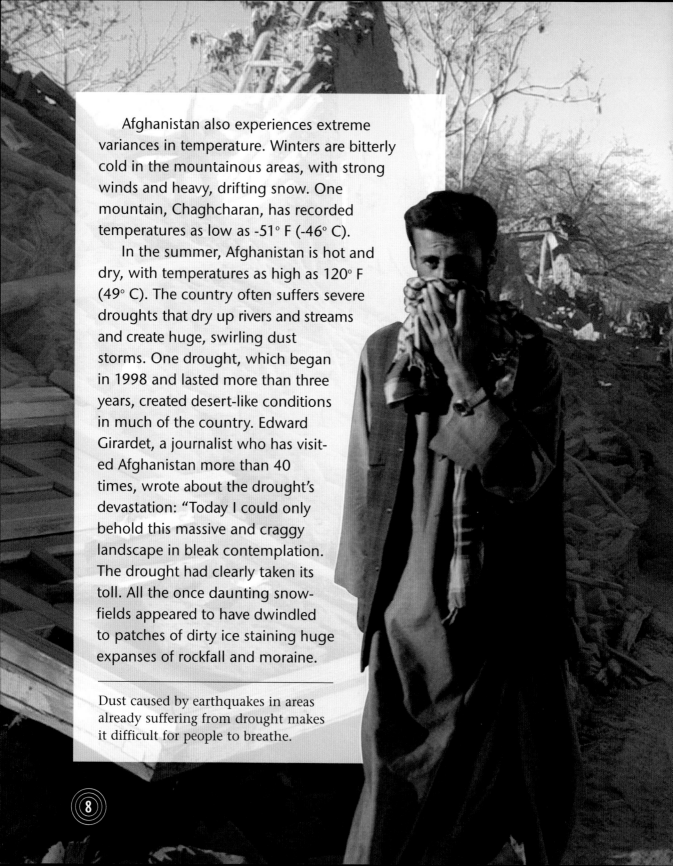

Afghanistan also experiences extreme variances in temperature. Winters are bitterly cold in the mountainous areas, with strong winds and heavy, drifting snow. One mountain, Chaghcharan, has recorded temperatures as low as -51° F (-46° C).

In the summer, Afghanistan is hot and dry, with temperatures as high as 120° F (49° C). The country often suffers severe droughts that dry up rivers and streams and create huge, swirling dust storms. One drought, which began in 1998 and lasted more than three years, created desert-like conditions in much of the country. Edward Girardet, a journalist who has visited Afghanistan more than 40 times, wrote about the drought's devastation: "Today I could only behold this massive and craggy landscape in bleak contemplation. The drought had clearly taken its toll. All the once daunting snow-fields appeared to have dwindled to patches of dirty ice staining huge expanses of rockfall and moraine.

Dust caused by earthquakes in areas already suffering from drought makes it difficult for people to breathe.

Even the once vividly green alpine pastures emerged as little more than dusty brushworks of brown. While I could still see clusters of glistening lakes with small streams and rivers trickling their way down into the valleys, many others were dry."[2]

The People of Afghanistan

In addition to natural disasters such as earthquakes and drought, Afghanistan's people have suffered other hardships as well. The country has been in a continuous state of conflict since the 1970s, and millions of Afghans have been forced to leave their homes. Some have moved to other parts of Afghanistan, and many others have fled to the neighboring countries of Pakistan and Iran. Countless others have died of starvation or disease, or have been killed as a result of war. Overall, the life expectancy for Afghans is only 46.2 years, and the country's infant mortality rate—the number of babies who do not survive—is one of the highest in the world.

The total population in Afghanistan is about 25 million people. There are many different ethnic groups in the country. Most of these groups are divided into separate tribes, each with its own rules and customs. The largest ethnic group, the Pashtuns, generally live in the southern and eastern parts of Afghanistan and speak the Pashtu language. The second largest ethnic group is the Tajiks, a non-tribal group. Most Tajiks live in the north and the west, and their language is Dari (Persian). Other ethnic groups include the Hazaras, Uzbeks, Baluchis, Turkmen, and Aimaqs. Most Afghans speak either Pashtu or Dari, but as many as 40 different languages and dialects are spoken in the country.

Since the 1970s, millions of Afghans have been forced to go to refugee camps such as this one in Mazar-e-Sharif.

An Islamic Nation

Although Afghans differ in their ethnic backgrounds and languages, almost all of them share the same religion—Islam. A person who practices the Islamic faith is called a Muslim. For spiritual guidance, Muslims rely on a holy book called the Koran, and they worship in mosques. The famous Blue Mosque, located in the northern Afghanistan city of Mazar-e Sharif, is one of the country's most treasured landmarks.

The Blue Mosque is one of Afghanistan's most treasured landmarks.

For centuries, the Islamic faith has played an important part in the cultural and social identity of Afghanistan's people. Muslims are strongly influenced by their faith in family and community relationships, as well as most other aspects of their lives.

Struggle for Survival

Of the estimated 25 million people in Afghanistan, more than four-fifths live in rural areas, and approximately one-fifth are nomads, or people who move constantly from place to place. The country is mountainous and rugged, so travel is difficult. As a result, many villages are independent and self-sufficient. The people build their own houses, grow whatever crops they can, and protect their communities. In many areas, communication systems are poor or even nonexistent, so residents may have little or no contact with people of other villages.

Afghans who can afford to buy food often make their purchases in outdoor markets.

Some Afghans still farm for a living, although this is more difficult than ever before. Only about 12 percent of Afghanistan's land is suitable for cultivation because water is in such short supply, but much of that land is now useless. Years of severe drought have destroyed farmland that was once rich and productive. In addition, deadly land mines—left over from years of war—still litter the ground.

Afghans who can afford to buy food usually buy it from street carts or in outdoor markets called bazaars. Most people, however, eat only food that they can grow themselves, and thousands rely on food that is donated by international relief agencies. It is not uncommon for poor families to make pots of soup from a single onion and potato, and to eat weeks-old bread that is softened with tea.

Modern conveniences that are taken for granted in other areas of the world are nonexistent in many parts of Afghanistan. Afghans who live in rural areas have primitive outhouses rather than bathrooms, and their only water comes from open wells that are often polluted. Most people have no electricity and have to rely on oil lamps for light. Luxuries such as automobiles, televisions, and telephones are rare, and only a fraction of Afghans can afford to own them.

In spite of their poverty, natural disasters, famine, and war, Afghans are proud, independent people. They value family pride, loyalty, and courage more than material possessions, and they are strongly devoted to their Islamic faith. Afghans are also known for their warmth and hospitality toward strangers—even those from faraway countries. Girardet recalls how they treated him whenever he visited: "You'd arrive in town bone tired and be welcomed and taken to a guest room with cushions—offered tea, sweets, and nuts. ... Even the poorest of Afghans had a sense of pride, great hospitality, so to me they were never poor."[3]

Afghanistan's History

The people of Afghanistan are part of a history that traces back to ancient times. The country's location, at the crossroads of Central, West, and South Asia, made it a desirable route for people who traveled across the Middle East. Some of these people chose to settle in Afghanistan, which is why there are so many different ethnic groups and tribes. Others were powerful conquerors who wanted to claim the land and expand their empires.

This painting depicts Alexander the Great's defeat of King Darius III in 650 B.C.

Conquest and Violence

One of Afghanistan's first conquerors was a Persian king named Darius I, who led his army through the Hindu Kush Mountains in 500 B.C., and conquered areas in the north and east. One hundred fifty years later, Alexander the Great of Macedon defeated the army of King Darius III and claimed Afghanistan as part of his empire.

In the third century B.C., the country was claimed by an Indian emperor named Aśoka. He had long been known as a famous warrior and ruthless conqueror, but once he embraced the religion of Buddhism, he became an advocate of peace. It was because of Aśoka that Buddhism made its way into Afghanistan, and it remained the dominant religion for hundreds of years.

In A.D. 642, Arab Muslim armies invaded Afghanistan, and by the mid-800s, Islam had replaced Buddhism as the primary religion. In 1220, a fierce Mongolian warrior named Genghis Khan set out to create an empire that stretched from China to the Caspian Sea. Accompanied by nearly 100,000 soldiers, Genghis Khan destroyed many of Afghanistan's cities and brutally murdered thousands of people.

One hundred years later, another Mongol conqueror, Timur, was known to be as cruel as Genghis Khan, and was famous for the towers he built from the skulls of people he had killed. Years later, his descendents rebuilt the Afghani cities Timur had destroyed and constructed shrines, mosques, and medresses (Islamic colleges). This period, known as the Timurid Era, was a time of great prosperity and cultural awareness.

Afghanistan Becomes a Nation

From the early 1500s to the mid-1700s, fierce territorial battles were common in Afghanistan as India and Persia fought over control of the land. In the mid-1740s, for the first time in history, the Pashtuns and other Afghani tribes united. An assembly of Pashtun tribal chiefs elected Ahmad Khan Abdali as their shah (the Persian word for "king"), and crowned him in a ceremony near the city of Kandahar. The new shah assumed the name Durrani, which meant "Pearl of Pearls." In 1747, he established Afghanistan as an official nation.

Throughout his reign, Ahmad Shah Durrani continued to expand his kingdom as he acquired territories from Persia to India. He consolidated the separate provinces of Afghanistan into one unified country, and ruled with the help of a council of tribal chiefs. This meant that even though Ahmad Shah was the country's leader, each tribal chief continued to rule his own tribe—an arrangement that was popular with Afghanistan's people. By the time of his death in 1772, Ahmad Shah had become known as a great leader.

Disintegration of an Empire

The years that followed the shah's death were turbulent ones. He had not named an heir, and his sons battled over who would take their father's place as king. Disputes over family and tribal issues continued over the next 50 years. By 1818, Ahmad Shah's empire had crumbled, and Afghanistan was no longer a unified nation. The next year, the country erupted in a civil war that lasted until 1826.

It was during this time that Great Britain and Russia began to grow more interested in Afghanistan. Both countries were powerful, and both controlled areas in central Asia. As each continued to acquire new territories, they seized land that had been part of Afghanistan. The power struggle between Russia and Great Britain, which was later termed the Great Game, was the beginning of political turbulence that lasted for many decades.

CHAPTER TWO

Political Turmoil

By the mid-1830s, Great Britain had become more aggressive in its desire for political control in Afghanistan. This led to British invasions in 1839 and 1878, which resulted in two long and bloody Anglo-Afghan Wars. Afghanistan remained independent, but Great Britain did not give up.

Amanullah Khan became emir (leader) in 1919, and he vowed to free his country from British influence. He ordered an attack on British troops in India, which began the third Anglo-Afghan War. Less than a year later, Great Britain signed a treaty that declared Afghanistan politically independent.

After the war ended, Amanullah vowed to modernize his country. He began to support radical policies that would change many of Afghanistan's centuries-old traditions and customs. To Afghans, these policies—such as less power for religious and tribal leaders and more rights for women—were shocking and unacceptable. In early 1929,

---

Opposite page: Emir Amanullah Khan's troops defeated the British in Kabul, Afghanistan, in the early 1900s.

Left: Mohammad Nadir became king after Khan was forced from the throne.

Afghanistan's tribal and religious leaders revolted against Amanullah and forced him from his throne. Later that year, Mohammad Nadir became king. He adopted a new constitution and began a program of gradual reform, but he was assassinated before he could implement many of his policies. His son, Mohammad Zahir Shah, assumed the throne and remained in power for the next 40 years.

A Decade of Stability

By the early 1950s, Afghanistan had joined the United Nations and had strengthened its relationships with the United States and many Western European countries. Zahir Shah's mission was to transform Afghanistan from a backward nation into one that was modern and prosperous. In 1964, he summoned a group of more than 400 tribal leaders, religious figures, and intellectuals to a council meeting called a *jirga*. The group created and ratified a constitution that formed a new government, promoted new freedoms, and guaranteed basic rights for Afghanistan's people.

The Advent of Communism

At about the same time that the new government was formed, another group also came together: the People's Democratic Party of Afghanistan (PDPA). The PDPA's philosophies were rooted in Communism, a system in which all property is owned and controlled by the government. The PDPA knew that a Communist system would not be well received by Afghanistan's people, so it kept PDPA's true mission a secret. Publicly, the PDPA stated that Communism was not its goal. In reality, however, the PDPA had the full support of the Soviet Union in its quest to establish a Communist government.

In 1973, while Zahir Shah was in Europe, a group of military officials stripped him of his power and named his cousin, Mohammad Dauod, president. Zahir went into exile in Italy, and Dauod abolished the royal kingdom and declared Afghanistan a republic.

King Mohammad Zahir Shah was in power for 40 years.

Dauod had previously supported the PDPA, but he was not in favor of the group's Communist beliefs. He worked to reduce PDPA's influence within the government. He also began to establish closer ties with other Islamic countries, which he believed would lessen Afghanistan's financial dependence on the Soviet Union. As a result, Dauod's relationship with the Soviet Union, and the PDPA, became very strained.

In 1978, a group of PDPA members assassinated Dauod and assumed political control. The group then passed a series of social and economic policies that were not popular with Afghanistan's people. Those who criticized the policies were seen as enemies of the government, and over the next year, PDPA leaders used violent force against protestors. They arrested and executed thousands of Afghans, including non-Muslims, religious leaders, political figures, and teachers. This violence caused mass riots in Afghanistan. People took to the streets with weapons such as machetes, swords, old guns, and wooden sticks, and they burned government buildings, tanks, and armored vehicles.

In an attempt to restore law and order, PDPA leaders bombed entire cities and executed thousands of rebels. Afghans continued to resist, however, and the new government realized it was in trouble. It turned to the Soviet Union for help.

A Decade of Terror

On December 24, 1979, the Soviet Union moved thousands of troops into Afghanistan and put its own Communist president, Babrak Karmal, in power. Over the next nine years, the Soviets occupied Afghanistan and virtually closed the country to the outside world. They took control of all newspapers, magazines, and book publishers. They arrested, imprisoned, and executed massive numbers of Afghans. They bombed cities and wiped out entire villages. To spread their destruction, they planted millions of land mines throughout the country. All in all, more than 1 million Afghans were killed during the Soviet occupation, and another 6 million fled for Pakistan and Iran, or sought shelter in Afghani refugee camps.

Mohammad Hassan Kakar, a professor who immigrated to the United States from Afghanistan, wrote about the consequences of the Soviet invasion: "Many thousands of Afghans perished … common sense should have persuaded the [Soviet] decision makers to stop the destruction and let the Afghans live the way they pleased, but they did so only in 1989, after almost ten years of war. By that time every ninth Afghan had died, every seventh (or eighth) had been disabled, and every third had fled abroad. Afghanistan lay in ruins."[4]

As the fighting continued, a group of Muslims formed a rebel force known as the Mujahideen. This group included thousands of Muslim guerrillas (rebel fighters) from countries outside of Afghanistan. Among these guerrillas was a wealthy Saudi Arabian Muslim named Osama bin Laden. He recruited soldiers to join the Mujahideen, built training camps for rebel recruits, and furnished them with money, equipment, and weapons.

Many Afghans were killed, wounded, or maimed as a result of the Soviet Union's occupation of Afghanistan.

WOMEN'S RIGHTS: BEFORE & AFTER THE TALIBAN

During the reign of the Taliban, life was extremely difficult for the people of Afghanistan. For the country's women, however, life was unbearable. Afghani women had no personal freedom, no rights, and no control over their lives. They were only allowed to appear in public if they wore *burqas*, which covered them from head to toe. Even then, they were forbidden to appear in public without a male escort. Women were not allowed to wear high heels, fingernail polish, or lipstick. They could not attend school, nor could they send their daughters to school. They could not leave their homes to work, and they were required to paint the windows of their homes so that when they were inside, no one on the outside could see them.

Sally Armstrong is a Canadian journalist who visited the city of Kandahar during the winter of 2001. She met and became friends with five Afghani women who confided in her about the horrors of life under Taliban rule. One year later, Armstrong returned to Afghanistan. In a June 2002 article in *Maclean's* magazine, she describes her amazement at how things had changed once the Taliban was no longer in control: "While the vast majority of women still wore burkas, change was clearly happening. ... Forced to wear wedge-heeled shoes during the Taliban era, and forbidden to wear white socks or any other form of stocking that might attract attention, the women of Kabul were making a statement, feet-first. Platform shoes, high heels, patent-leather pumps were everywhere. And hosiery was patterned, coloured and very much on display. ... Hands, formerly hidden, were very much in evidence while women walked together, talking, gesturing, and even returning the thumbs-up

After the Taliban lost control of Afghanistan, women were able to register for classes at Kabul University.

sign to me when we passed on the street. There was a palpable air of excitement in the city— and music, which also had been forbidden, was playing at every little kiosk. Women were working again ... girls' schools had re-opened ... and the girls were writing entrance exams to get back to university."

Armstrong traveled to Kandahar to find the women with whom she had become friends a year before. She describes their reunion as "wonderful, exhilarating, and very emotional." No longer filled with fear and dread, the women shared their hopes for the future. They told Armstrong they wanted to travel, see foreign countries, and to get an education. More than anything else, they looked forward to peace and freedom.

When it was time for Armstrong to say goodbye to her friends and return home, they posed for a photograph together. The last words they said to her undoubtedly speak for many women in Afghanistan: "This time you can use our family names and our faces. We're safe now. We're not afraid anymore."

The Soviets found the rebel fighters to be both tough and dangerous. Soon, the Mujahideen became more organized and aggressive, and it fought back with sophisticated weapons furnished by the United States and other non-Communist countries. Finally, the Mujahideen was able to drive the Soviets out of Afghanistan. In 1988, representatives from Afghanistan, the United States, the Soviet Union, and Pakistan signed an agreement in Geneva, Switzerland, that guaranteed the removal of all Soviet troops.

After the Soviets had withdrawn, the Communist Party remained in power until 1992, when it was overthrown by the Mujahideen. In the following years, conflicts and battles over ethnic, territorial, and political issues grew worse, and the Mujahideen factions that had united to fight the Soviets began to fight among themselves. Once again, the country was embroiled in a bloody civil war. By 1995, approximately one-third of the country had been destroyed, and millions of Afghans were dead, injured, or displaced from their homes.

The Rise of the Taliban

After nearly two decades of war and destruction, the people of Afghanistan were desperate for peace and stability. So, when a group of radical Muslims, many of whom were ex-Mujahideen members, emerged and promised to restore peace, many Afghans welcomed them. This group was known as the Taliban.

The Taliban leaders had a goal: to assume complete control of Afghanistan's government. They knew, however, that they could not achieve this goal without the people's support. To gain it, they promised Afghans that the Taliban's only interest was to end the violence and restore peace, and not to pursue political power or control the

A string of prisoners awaits punishment by the Taliban. Under the Taliban, thousands of Afghans were beaten, imprisoned, and killed.

government. Neamatollah Nojumi, an Afghan who fought with the Mujahideen, explains: "The call for peace and security and an end to the civil war was a long desire for Afghans inside and outside, and this declaration was a perfect match. ... Years of civil war and the bloody clashes between the ex-Mujahideen groups in Kabul had disturbed the lives of millions of Afghans and made them desperate for peace and security."[5]

By 1996, it had become obvious that the Taliban had lied to Afghanistan's people. Once again, Afghans became the victims of a domineering, brutal style of leadership. The Taliban enlisted thousands of enforcers to patrol the streets and monitor people's behavior. These enforcers carried large sticks, and they were given the authority to beat anyone who disobeyed the Taliban's rigid and oppressive rules. People were not allowed to listen to music or to own televisions, VCRs, or cameras. Men were forbidden to shave or trim their beards, and women were not allowed to appear in public unless they were covered with head-to-toe garments called *burqas*. Women were forbidden to talk to

AHMAD SHAH MASSOUD: A FALLEN HERO

Ahmad Shah Massoud first made a name for himself during the Soviet occupation of Afghanistan. As a commander of the Mujahideen resistance fighters, he was known as a brilliant, respected leader, as well as a brave fighter. His skill and intelligence as a Mujahideen commander earned him the

Afghan national hero Ahmad Shah Massoud (right) was killed by suicide bombers in 2001.

nickname "Lion of Panjsher," because he successfully defied Soviet attempts to conquer his Panjsher Valley in Northern Afghanistan. Massoud was a man who never stopped believing in freedom and independence, and he refused to give up the fight against the Soviets. Eventually, his bravery and determination paid off. After nine years of occupation by the Soviet Union, he and his fellow Mujahideen forced the Soviets out of Afghanistan.

After the Soviets were gone, a Communist government remained, and Massoud vowed to continue the fight for Afghanistan's independence. In 1992, he thought he had accomplished his goal. The Mujahideen captured Kabul, and Massoud became the defense minister. However, the various factions that made up the Mujahideen began to fight each other over control of Kabul, and Massoud could not control them. A civil war broke out, and after the deaths of thousands of Afghans, and the destruction of

Kabul, the Taliban took over the capital city. Massoud was forced to return to his base in Panjsher.

In 1999, Massoud formed a resistance movement called the Northern Alliance. Once again, he built a reputation as a brave fighter and a fearless leader. He was not afraid to stand up to the Taliban, a group he believed was focused on control and oppression. Over the next few years, Massoud negotiated with Taliban members, and insisted that they arrive at a political compromise that benefited Afghanistan's people. Because of this, he became known as a true Afghani hero.

On September 9, 2001, Ahmad Shah Massoud was killed by two suicide bombers who posed as journalists. His death brought shock and sadness to the people of Afghanistan, as well as to others around the world who knew what he stood for: peace, independence, and freedom. To honor him, and to keep his memory alive, Massoud was officially named the national hero of Afghanistan on April 25, 2002.

For years, Taliban soldiers like these terrorized nearly three quarters of the Afghani population.

men in public, to go to school, or to work outside the home. No one was allowed to laugh in public. All recreational activities were forbidden, and Afghans—who are by nature hospitable people—were not allowed to have foreign visitors in their homes.

The Beginning of the End

By the end of 1996, the Taliban controlled approximately three-fourths of Afghanistan, and it continued to unleash its reign of terror on the country's people. Under the Taliban, thousands of Afghans were beaten, imprisoned, and killed. Entire cities and towns were destroyed, and houses and other buildings were burned to the ground. Non-Muslims were executed in the name of "ethnic cleansing," because they were seen as infidels, or people who did not practice the Islamic faith. Hundreds of thousands of Afghans abandoned their homes and escaped to neighboring countries.

As the Taliban continued to exercise its rigid control and authority, an anti-Taliban resistance group called the Northern Alliance began to grow more powerful. The group, led by former Mujahideen fighter Ahmed Shah Massoud, fought the Taliban. It made significant progress as it worked to defeat the Taliban and decrease the regime's power.

The turning point came on September 11, 2001. Muslim terrorists used American planes to attack the World Trade Center in New York City and the Pentagon in Washington, D.C., and thousands of people were killed. Osama bin Laden, leader of the terrorist group al-Qaeda, claimed responsibility for the attack on the United States—and bin Laden was closely tied to the Taliban.

After the terrorist attacks, the United States demanded that the Taliban turn bin Laden over, but the Taliban refused. To retaliate, and to force the Taliban out of power, the United States joined with the Northern Alliance and a coalition of several other nations in a fight against terrorism. Sites throughout Afghanistan that were suspected hiding places and terrorist training camps were destroyed in a series of bombing attacks. British and U.S. soldiers combed the mountains and caves in search of Taliban members, as well as Osama bin Laden and members of al-Qaeda. By the end of 2001, the Taliban had been defeated, and many of its leaders had been captured and arrested. Bin Laden remained at large.

After the Taliban was ousted from power, Northern Alliance leaders and other Afghan representatives met in Germany. They discussed what kind of government the country should have, and selected a temporary president, Hamid Karzai. The group scheduled a future *jirga* to elect a permanent president, draft a constitution, and create their new government.

CHAPTER THREE

Looking to the Future

No one knows for sure what tomorrow will bring for Afghanistan, but its future looks bleak. Years of war, death, and destruction have left much of the country in ruins. Highways, bridges, and buildings have been demolished. Farms and orchards have been destroyed. Villages that were once alive with activity have become ghost towns. Deadly land mines cover miles of Afghanistan's landscape, and remnants of U.S. cluster bombs remain on the ground.

Experts say that it could take more than a decade to rebuild Afghanistan—and much longer for the country to recover from so many years of constant turmoil.

Political changes

After years of oppression and instability in Afghanistan's government, most Afghans remain distrustful of political authority. Throughout history, the only effective Afghani leaders have been those who understood the importance of the different ethnic groups and tribes. These groups, such as the Pashtuns, the Tajiks, the Hazaras, and others, have always had their own ideas about how Afghanistan should be governed. When they have been ignored, and their opinions have not been taken into

After the terrorist attacks against the United States on September 11, 2001, the U.S. Army went to Afghanistan to search for al-Qaeda leader Osama bin Laden.

consideration, these groups have rebelled. The result has been a state of turmoil that has existed for centuries.

In the summer of 2002, Afghanistan's President Karzai and other leaders held a *loya jirga*, or "grand council" meeting, in Kabul. The meeting was attended by 1,500 Afghani representatives, one of whom was Zahir Shah, who returned to Afghanistan after nearly 30 years in exile. The group elected Karzai as president, and determined that he would lead the country until 2003, when a national election would be held.

Many Afghans saw the *loya jirga* and Karzai's election as signs of a better future, and they were hopeful about the country's new leadership. There were others, however, who were not happy about the new president. Rival tribes continued to fight over power and control, and violence erupted frequently. Then, less than a month after Karzai took office, the vice president, Haji Abdul Qadir, was shot to death outside his government office.

Hamid Karzai was elected as Afghanistan's president in 2002.

Fifteen hundred Afghani delegates attended the *loya jirga*, or "grand council," in Kabul in the summer of 2002.

OSAMA BIN LADEN

He is called many different things. Most Americans call him a terrorist, while his followers call him a hero. Journalists have referred to him as the mysterious Saudi, an Islamic extremist, or the most dangerous man in the world. His name is Osama bin Laden, and no matter how people refer to him, he has become one of the most notorious villains of all time.

Osama bin Laden was born in Saudi Arabia in 1957, to a Syrian mother and a Yemeni father. His father's construction business was extremely successful—so much so that his family had become one of the wealthiest, most powerful families in the Saudi kingdom. When bin Laden was thirteen, his father died in a helicopter crash, and the boy inherited a fortune worth millions of dollars. He later attended college, and in 1979 he earned a degree in civil engineering.

In the same year that bin Laden graduated from college, the Soviet Union invaded Afghanistan. He was determined to fight a Communist takeover of the country, and he began to use his own money, plus millions more that he raised, to recruit, train, and arm members of the Mujahideen in their fight against the Soviets. Bin Laden set up training camps for the soldiers, and formed a group called al-Qaeda, which is Arabic for "The Base." In 1989, the Soviet Union withdrew its army from Afghanistan. Bin Laden called the Soviet defeat a victory for all Muslims—he also said it was a sign that even superpowers are vulnerable when the will to defeat them is strong enough.

In 1991, bin Laden was asked to leave his native country because he had repeatedly spoken against its government. Shortly after that, thousands of American troops arrived in Saudi Arabia for the Persian Gulf War, and bin Laden was enraged. He believed that the U.S. presence in Saudi Arabia was no different from the

Soviet Union's occupation of Afghanistan. He had always felt hostile toward America, but after the Gulf War, his hostility turned to hatred. Osama bin Laden vowed revenge.

Over the next several years, bin Laden developed al-Qaeda into a worldwide terrorist organization. He became internationally known as a criminal, and a number of violent terrorist attacks were linked to him and al-Qaeda. These included the 1993 bombing of New York's World Trade Center, and the bombing of two U.S. military installations in Saudi Arabia in 1995 and 1996. In 1998, the American embassies in Kenya and Tanzania (Africa) were bombed, and in 2000, an American ship was bombed in Yemen. As with the others, these attacks were linked to bin Laden.

On September 11, 2001, terrorists used American jets to attack the United States, and Osama bin Laden was immediately the number-one suspect. During an October 2001 interview with the Arabic network, al-Jazeera, he

Osama bin Laden admitted he was involved in the September 11, 2001, terrorist attacks against the United States.

admitted his involvement, and said: "We believe that the defeat of America is possible, with the help of God, and is even easier for us—God permitting—than the defeat of the Soviet Union was before."

Continued Threats

Qadir's assassination was a sign that violence and unrest are still very much alive in Afghanistan, even without the Taliban in power. There are Islamic extremists in the country who sympathize with Osama bin Laden and the Taliban, and there are people who resent the United States for its military intervention in Afghanistan. These people vow to retaliate with

Warlords threaten the stability of Afghanistan.

Afghans staged a peace demonstration in Kabul after the Taliban had been ousted from power in 2001.

future terrorist attacks, such as those that occurred on September 11, 2001. They also continue to threaten Afghani people who are supportive of the United States' presence in Afghanistan.

Another major problem in Afghanistan is its warlords. Unlike tribal leaders, who are chosen by the people, a warlord is someone who simply claims a particular territory for his own. As the Taliban began to lose control of Afghanistan's cities and towns, warlords rushed in to claim them and expand the areas they controlled.

While the Taliban was in power, many warlords were part of the Northern Alliance, and considered the Taliban their enemy. Others were—and continue to be—Taliban supporters. Most warlords are described as ruthless, power-hungry, and brutal toward anyone who opposes them or stands in the way of their control over their region. *Wall Street Journal* writer Nancy DeWolf Smith says that warlords are "thugs" who are a real threat to Afghanistan's stability: "Warlords ... don't just fade away. Unless they are confronted by a determined united front of Afghans and genuine foreign friends, many of them will continue to threaten the peace in Afghanistan, and thus keep the wounds open for more maggots of terrorism."[6]

New Hope for the People

In spite of how dismal Afghanistan's current situation is, the Afghani people are more optimistic than they have been for many years. Once again, there is music, laughter, and freedom in this war-torn country— things that people in other countries take for granted, but are precious to the people of Afghanistan. Afghans who were forced to flee to neighboring countries or leave their villages for refugee camps have begun to return to their homes in the hope that peace will reign at last. Such is the case with Ahmad Hussein, a 12-year-old Afghan boy, who says: "My greatest wish is to be happy, to learn to read and write, to have warm shoes and eat as much as I want to. I want to return home."[7]

President Karzai says his goal is to bring unity to a country that for so many years has been divided by war, violence, anger, and rivalries: "There is bitterness. There is resentment, of course that is there. I have resentment too, as an individual, but then we must put that resentment behind us. ... Look at this country now. We are again now a country where we all have a sense of belonging. The former king is here, the common refugee is here. ... We must go hand in hand to build this country."[8]

After the fall of the Taliban, music was allowed at celebrations.

For Afghanistan, the past has been filled with years of turmoil, violence, and pain. Yet no matter how bleak the present may seem, there is still hope for the future. Perhaps this is best described by a woman who has witnessed not just the country's dark side, but also its beauty, as well as the amazing courage and strength of its people:

> For some, there's a magic in the sweep of open country; for others it's the sweet smell of the almond blossoms in the night's soft breezes; or the special relationships with its people. But for everyone there's one vision that can never be forgotten. . . . For a few weeks each year when the howl of winter's bitter winds subsides, spring comes. . . . The rivers overflow with lifegiving waters. Against a carpet of green, the tulips unfold their waxy petals. . . . Poppies, lilies, hyacinths, and roses lift their pure faces to the crystal clear sky. . . . As surely as day becomes night, spring's beauty returns. . . . There is something revealing in this victory of life over [Afghanistan's] severe obstacles. In it, I believe, the people of this troubled land today can find the strength and hope they need to endure.[9]

Poppies bloom each spring in Afghanistan.

Important Dates

500 B.C.	Persian King Darius I conquers what is now Afghanistan
327 B.C.	Alexander the Great defeats the army of King Darius III and claims Afghanistan as part of his empire
260 B.C.	Emperor Aśoka introduces Buddhism to Afghanistan
A.D. 642	Arab Muslim armies invade Afghanistan and introduce the Islam religion
1220	Mongolian warrior Genghis Khan conquers Afghanistan; cities are destroyed and thousands of people are killed
1370	Timur, another Mongolian conqueror, brings death and destruction to Afghanistan
1747	An assembly of tribal chiefs elects Ahmad Khan Abdali as shah; Abdali assumes the name Durrani and establishes Afghanistan as an official nation
1819 – 1826	Afghani civil war
1839	British troops invade Afghanistan
1839 – 1842	First Anglo-Afghan War
1878 – 1880	Second Anglo-Afghan War
1919	Amanullah Khan becomes Afghanistan's emir; orders attack on British troops in India; third Anglo-Afghan War ends and a treaty is signed with Great Britain that declares Afghanistan politically independent
1929	Afghanistan's tribal and religious leaders force Amanullah Khan from the throne; nine months later, Mohammad Nadir Khan becomes king
1933	Mohammad Nadir is assassinated; his son, Mohammad Zahir Shah, assumes the throne and remains in power for 40 years
1946	Afghanistan is admitted to the United Nations
1964	Zahir Shah hosts a *jirga*; a new constitution is approved

1965	First secret assembly of the People's Democratic Party of Afghanistan (PDPA) is held by its founding members
1973	Mohammad Dauod takes control of the government and establishes himself as president; Zahir Shah is forced into exile in Italy
1978	PDPA members and Islamic fundamentalists assassinate Dauod and take control of the government; massive riots erupt throughout Afghanistan
1979	Soviet Union invades Afghanistan with thousands of troops
1988	Representatives from Afghanistan, the United States, the Soviet Union, and Pakistan sign agreement in Geneva, Switzerland, to guarantee removal of Soviet troops from Afghanistan
1992	Mujahideen overthrows Afghanistan's Communist government
1994	Radical Islamic group, the Taliban, establishes administration in the city of Kandahar and begins campaign to expand its control
1996	Taliban captures control of Kabul, Afghanistan's capital city; by the end of the year, the Taliban controls approximately three-fourths of the country
2001	World Trade Center in New York and Pentagon in Washington, D.C., are attacked by Muslim terrorists who hijack American planes; Saudi terrorist and leader of terrorist group al-Qaeda, Osama bin Laden, claims responsibility for attacks; U.S. demands that the Taliban release bin Laden are not met; in retaliation, U.S. bombs Afghanistan; Taliban is defeated and removed from power

For More Information

WEBSITES

Ask Asia

www.askasia.org

This is the official website for the Asia Society. Its purpose is to increase Americans' understanding of Asia.

CNNfyi.com

http://fyi.cnn.com/2001/fyi/news/10/23/afghanistan/index.html

A student news website that includes an interactive history lesson on Afghanistan.

CoolPlanet.com

www.oxfam.org.uk/coolplanet/kidsweb/world/Afghan/afghanhome.htm

This website includes historical, geographical, and societal information on Afghanistan and its people.

Lonely Planet

www.lonelyplanet.com/destinations/middle_east/afghanistan/index.htm

An informative website that focuses on travel in Afhanistan.

BOOKS

Mary Louise Clifford, *The Land and People of Afghanistan*. Philadelphia: J.B. Lippincott, 1962.

Leila Merrell Foster, *Afghanistan*. New York: Grolier, 1996.

Henry Gilfond, *Afghanistan*. New York: Franklin Watts, 1980.

PERIODICALS

"Facing the Future: The Women of Afghanistan Look Ahead," *Current Events*, March 8, 2002. An article about how life for Afghani women is different since the Taliban is no longer in power.

"The Most Dangerous Place on Earth: A Look Inside Afghanistan," *Current Events*, November 30, 2001. An article about the struggles in Afghanistan since ancient times.

Source Quotations

1. Rosanne Klass, *Land of the High Flags*. New York: Random House, 1964.
2. Edward Girardet, "Eyewitness: Afghanistan," *National Geographic*, December 2001, pp. 130–138.
3. Quoted in D.L. Parsell, "Afghanistan Reporter Looks Back on Two Decades of Change," *National Geographic News*, November 19, 2001. http://news.nationalgeographic.com
4. Mohammad Hassan Kakar, "Afghanistan: The Soviet Invasion and the Afghan Response" Afghanvoice.com. http://www.afghanvoice.com/afgsovinv.htm.
5. Neamatollah Nojumi, *The Rise of the Taliban in Afghanistan*. New York: Palgrave, 2002, pp. 134–135.
6. Nancy DeWolf Smith, "Get Rid of the Warlords," WSJ.com, January 28, 2002. http://www.opinionjournal.com/columnists/nsmith.
7. Quoted in Mir Hekmatullah Sadat, "Afghanistan's Internal Refugees: Trapped at the Margins," Afghanmagazine.com — Lemar-Aftaab, January-December 2001. http://www.afghanmagazine.com/2001/articles/internalrefugees.html
8. Quoted in Kathy Gannon, "Karzai Seeks to Unite Afghans," Afghanistan's website, June 27, 2002. http://www.afghanistans.com.
9. Jane R. McCauley/National Geographic Society, *Secret Corners of the World*. Washington, DC: National Geographic Society, 1982, p. 48.

About the Author

Peggy J. Parks holds a Bachelor of Science degree from Aquinas College in Grand Rapids, Michigan, where she graduated magna cum laude. She is a freelance writer who has written a number of titles for The Gale Group, including two for Lucent Books' Careers for the 21st Century series, one for Blackbirch Press's Giants of Science series, and three for KidHaven Press's Exploring Careers series. She was previously the profile writer for Towery Publications' *Grand Rapids: The City That Works*. Parks lives in Muskegon, Michigan, a town that she says inspires her writing because of its location on the shores of Lake Michigan.

Index

Afghanistan
  future, 33–39
  government, 21, 29, 31, 33
  history, 5, 14, 16–17
  language, 10
  people, 10-14
  political turmoil, 19–31
  religion, 12, 16
  weather, 4, 8
Alexander the Great, 16
Amanullah Khan, 19-20
Anglo-Afghan Wars, 19
Arab Muslims, 16
Aśoka, 16
Assassination, 34

bin Laden, Osama, 22, 29, 34–35, 36–37
Blue Mosque, 12
Bombing, 22, 29, 33, 37
Buddhism, 16
Burqas, 26, 28

China, 7, 16
Civil war, 5, 17, 24, 31
Communism, 5, 20–21, 22, 24, 31, 36
Conquests, 16
Coup, 5

Daoud, Mohammad, 21
Darius, 16
Desert, 8
Disease, 10
Drought, 4, 8, 10, 13
Durrani, Ahmad Shah, 17

Earthquakes, 4, 7, 10
Education, 26, 27
Embassies, U.S., 37
Ethnic cleansing, 28
Ethnic groups, 10, 14, 33
Executions, 21, 22
Exile, 21, 34
Extremists, 34, 36

Famine, 14
Farming, 13
Food, 13–14

Genghis Khan, 16
Great Britain, 17, 19
Great Game, 17
Guerillas, 22, 24
Gulf War, 36-37

Haji Abdul Qadir, 34
Hazaras, 10, 33
Hindu Kush mountains, 7, 16
History, 14, 16–17

India, 16–17, 19
Infidels, 28
Iran, 7, 10, 22
Islam, 4, 12, 14, 16, 28

Jirga, 20, 29, 34

Kabul, 26, 28, 31, 34
Kandahar, 17, 26, 27
Karmal, Babrak, 22
Karzai, Hamid, 29, 34, 38
Kenya, 37
Koran, 12

Land mines, 13, 22, 33

Language, 10
Loya jirga, 34

Massoud, Ahmad Shah, 29, 30–31
Mazar-e Sharif, 12
Middle East, 7, 14
Mosques, 12
Mujahideen, 22, 24, 28, 30–31, 36
Muslims, 12, 16, 22, 24, 29, 36

Nadir, Mohammad, 20
Natural disasters, 7, 8, 10, 14
Nomads, 12
Northern Alliance, 29, 31, 35

Pakistan, 7, 10, 22, 24
Pashtuns, 10, 17, 33
Peace, 16, 24, 25
People's Democratic Party of Afghanistan (PDPA), 20–21
Persia, 16–17
Persian Gulf War, 36–37
Politics, 19–31
Poverty, 14

al-**Q**aeda, 29, 36, 37

Rebels, 5, 21, 22, 24, 33
Refugees, 5, 22, 38
Relief agencies, 14
Religion, 12, 16
Riots, 21
Russia, 17

Saudi Arabia, 36–37

Schools, 26, 27
September 11, 2001, 29, 35, 37
Shah, 17
Soviet Union, 5, 7, 20–21, 22–24, 30–31, 36, 37
Starvation, 10

Tajiks, 10, 33
Taliban, 24–29, 31, 34–35
Tanzania, 37
Terrorism, 28, 29, 35, 36, 37
Timur, 16
Tribes, 10, 14, 17, 33

United Nations, 20
United States, 20, 24, 29, 33, 34–35
  and Persian Gulf War, 36–37

Violence, 5, 16, 21, 25, 34, 38

War, 10, 14, 19
Warlords, 35
Women, 19, 26–27, 28
World Trade Center, 29, 37

Yemen, 37

Zahir Shah, Mohammad, 20-21, 34